D1435515

This [illegible] belongs to

....

....

PUFFIN BOOKS

UK | USA | Canada | Ireland | Australia | India | New Zealand | South Africa

Puffin Books is part of the Penguin Random House group of companies whose addresses can be found at global.penguinrandomhouse.com

First published by Ladybird Books 2004
This edition published by Puffin Books 2017
001

Copyright © the Eric and Gillian Hill Family Trust, 2004

The moral right of the author/illustrator has been asserted

Manufactured in China

A CIP catalogue record for this book is available from the British Library

ISBN: 978–0–241–32647–3

All correspondence to:
Puffin Books, Penguin Random House Children's
80 Strand, London, WC2R 0RL

Spot's Show and Tell

Eric Hill

Spot and his friends arrived at school bright and early.

"Good morning, everyone,"
said Miss Bear.
"Good morning,
Miss Bear,"
everyone replied.

When everyone was settled, Miss Bear asked, "Does anyone have anything special for Show and Tell today?"

Helen and Tom both put their hands up.

Miss Bear asked Helen to come up first.

Helen held up her pink ballet shoes for everyone to see. They had lovely ribbons to keep them on her feet.

"Every week I go to ballet class," said Helen. "Next week we're doing a concert and I'm going to be a flower!"

Everyone thought Helen's ballet shoes were very special. They all clapped. Helen was very happy.

Next it was Tom's turn.
"I've brought my new kite," said Tom. "It's very special. My dad helped me to make it. We used special paper, wooden sticks and glue. We're going to fly it on Saturday."

Everyone thought Tom's kite was wonderful and they all clapped. Tom was very happy.

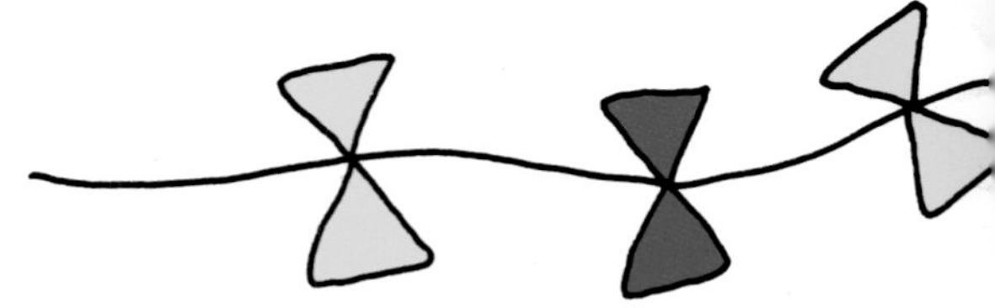

Later that morning, it was time for painting. Spot and Steve shared an easel.

"I'm going to bring something for Show and Tell tomorrow," said Spot.

"Me too," said Steve. "But I'm not sure what to bring."
"Neither am I," said Spot. "We'll have to think hard, won't we?"

That afternoon, Steve was going to Spot's house to play. Sally picked Spot and Steve up and they all walked home together.

Steve saw a bright orange autumn leaf on the grass and he picked it up.
“Maybe I’ll take this for Show and Tell tomorrow,” he said. “It’s a lovely colour!”

When they got back, Spot and Steve played cars in Spot's room.

"My car collection is special," Spot said to Steve. "Maybe I'll take my cars to Show and Tell tomorrow."

"That's a good idea," said Steve.

At bedtime, Spot was still thinking about Show and Tell.

Suddenly, he had a great idea. "I know what I want to take to Show and Tell tomorrow," said Spot. "It's very, very special." Spot whispered something to Sally.

"That sounds perfect!" said Sally, and she kissed Spot goodnight. "Sweet dreams, Spot!"

The next morning, Spot was smiling and cheerful when he met Steve on the way to school.

"Have you got something for Show and Tell?" asked Steve.

"Yes," said Spot. "And it's very, very special. Have you got something?"

"Yes," said Steve, happily. "And it's very special too."

At school, Miss Bear asked if anyone had brought something special for Show and Tell.

Spot and Steve put their hands up and Miss Bear asked them to come to the front of the class.

"I'd like to show the picture
I painted of my friend Spot!"
said Steve.

Spot laughed.
"And I'd like to show the picture
I painted of my friend Steve,"
said Spot.

Everyone clapped, even Miss Bear!
Spot and Steve were very,
very happy!

D1435520

52 THINGS TO DO
WHILE YOU SCREW

52 THINGS TO DO WHILE YOU SCREW
COPYRIGHT © GWION PRYDDERCH, 2018
ALL RIGHTS RESERVED.

NO PART OF THIS BOOK MAY BE REPRODUCED BY ANY MEANS, NOR TRANSMITTED, NOR TRANSLATED INTO A MACHINE LANGUAGE, WITHOUT THE WRITTEN PERMISSION OF THE PUBLISHERS.

GWION PRYDDERCH HAS ASSERTED HIS RIGHT TO BE IDENTIFIED AS THE AUTHOR OF THIS WORK IN ACCORDANCE WITH SECTIONS 77 AND 78 OF THE COPYRIGHT, DESIGNS AND PATENTS ACT 1988.

CONDITION OF SALE
THIS BOOK IS SOLD SUBJECT TO THE CONDITION THAT IT SHALL NOT, BY WAY OF TRADE OR OTHERWISE, BE LENT, RESOLD, HIRED OUT OR OTHERWISE CIRCULATED IN ANY FORM OF BINDING OR COVER OTHER THAN THAT IN WHICH IT IS PUBLISHED AND WITHOUT A SIMILAR CONDITION INCLUDING THIS CONDITION BEING IMPOSED ON THE SUBSEQUENT PURCHASER.

AN HACHETTE UK COMPANY
WWW.HACHETTE.CO.UK

SUMMERSDALE PUBLISHERS LTD
PART OF OCTOPUS PUBLISHING GROUP LIMITED
CARMELITE HOUSE
50 VICTORIA EMBANKMENT
LONDON
EC4Y 0DZ
UK

WWW.SUMMERSDALE.COM
PRINTED AND BOUND IN CHINA
ISBN: 978-1-78685-490-2

SUBSTANTIAL DISCOUNTS ON BULK QUANTITIES OF SUMMERSDALE BOOKS ARE AVAILABLE TO CORPORATIONS, PROFESSIONAL ASSOCIATIONS AND OTHER ORGANISATIONS. FOR DETAILS CONTACT GENERAL ENQUIRIES: TELEPHONE: +44 (0) 1243 771107 OR EMAIL: ENQUIRIES@SUMMERSDALE.COM.

52 THINGS TO DO WHILE YOU SCREW

HUGH JASSBURN

EVER THOUGHT YOU COULD DO WITH SOMETHING TO DO WHILE YOU'RE DOING IT? EVER NEEDED A BREATHER DURING A MARATHON SESSION? WELL, THIS IS THE BOOK FOR YOU – A COLLECTION OF NAUGHTY GAMES, FACTS AND QUOTES TO AMUSE THE BROADEST OF MINDS, ALONG WITH A FEW CHEEKY WORD SEARCHES TO GET YOU IN THE MOOD. THESE PRIVATE-TIME PUZZLES WILL KEEP YOU GOING FOR HOURS...

... WHILE YOU SCREW

YOU HAVE 15 SECONDS

FIND THIS PAIR ON THE OPPOSITE PAGE

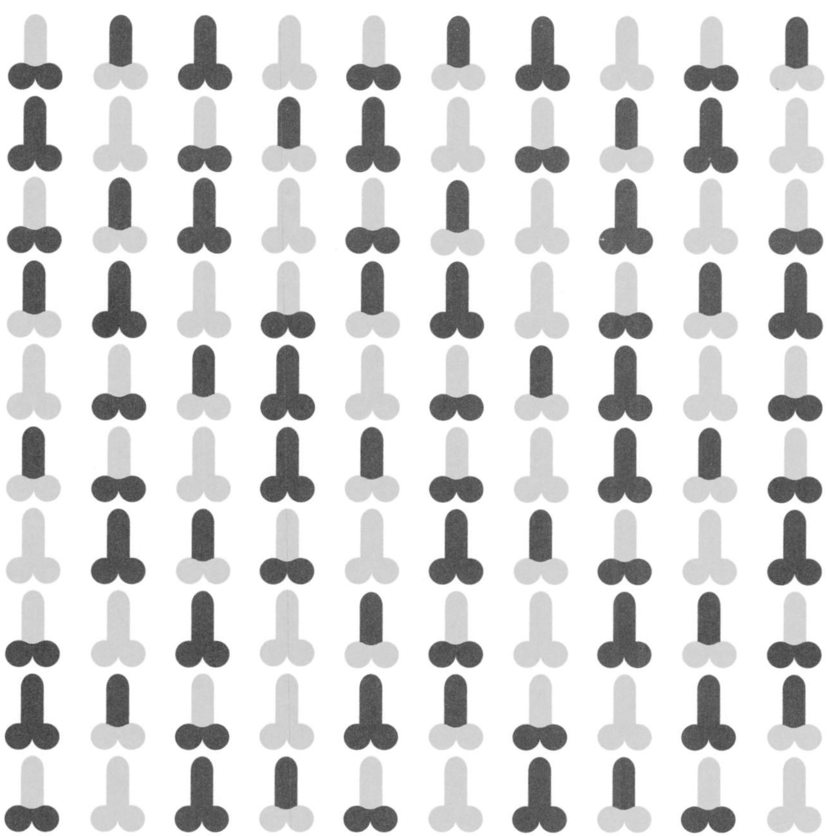

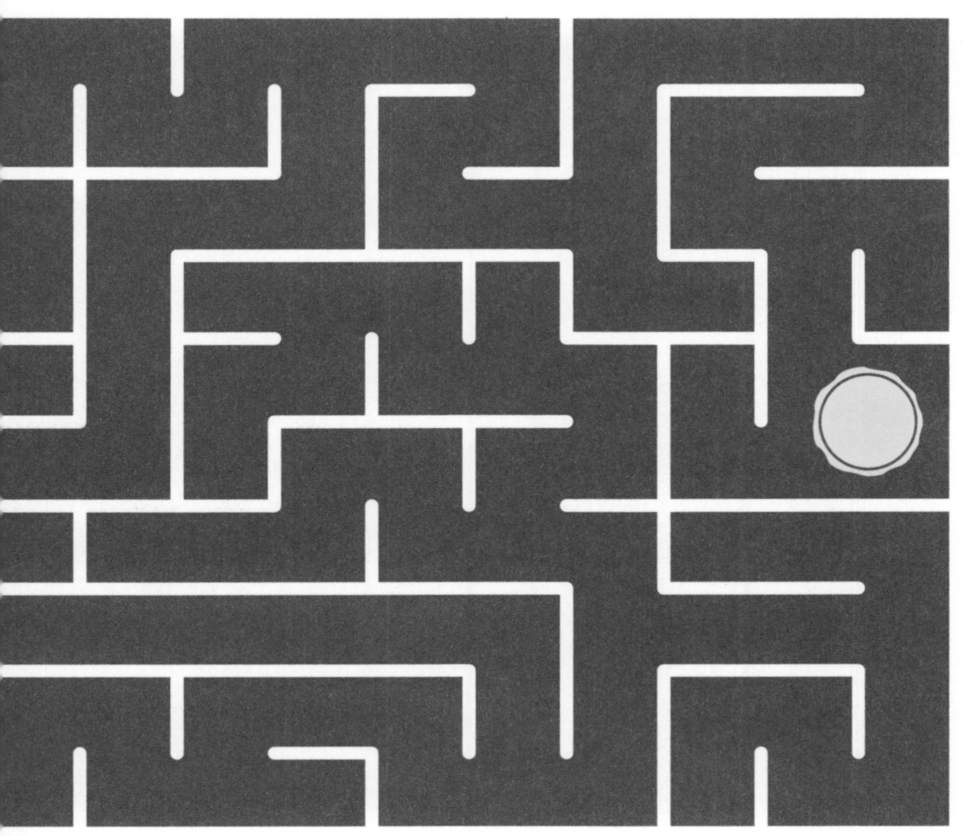

SCREW FACT

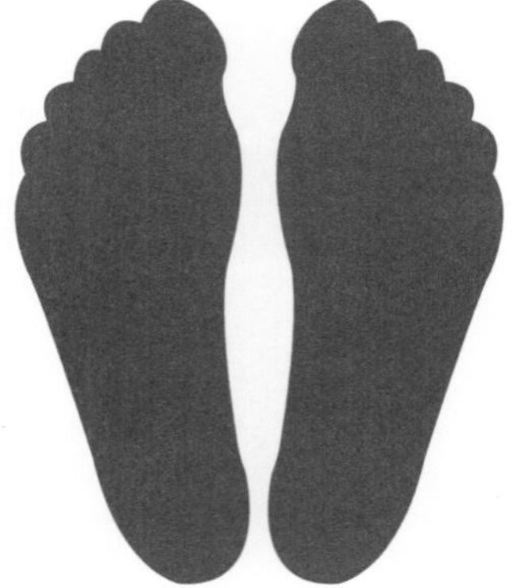

FEET AND SHOE FETISHES ARE THE MOST COMMON IN THE WESTERN WORLD

THE FRENCH TERM *LA PETITE MORT* REFERS TO AN ORGASM – IT TRANSLATES AS 'THE LITTLE DEATH'

PENIS
WILLY
DICK
PRICK
MEMBER
TOOL
COCK
KNOB
CHOPPER
WINKLE
PECKER

A W S E R T Y U I K

J W I L L Y K L C O

T H N G F D S I O A

O M E M B E R V C C

O B P N L P E M K R

L S D K F G P J L E

W E N R T Y P U I K

N I B V K N O B C C

W M H O I U H Y T E

N C W E D I C K R P

SEX IS LIKE AIR – IT'S NOT IMPORTANT UNLESS YOU AREN'T GETTING ANY

JOHN CALLAHAN

WELCOME TO

BENDOVA

A) CZECH REPUBLIC

B) MOLDOVA

C) ROMANIA

MIRROR POSITION

FIND THE MIRROR IMAGE

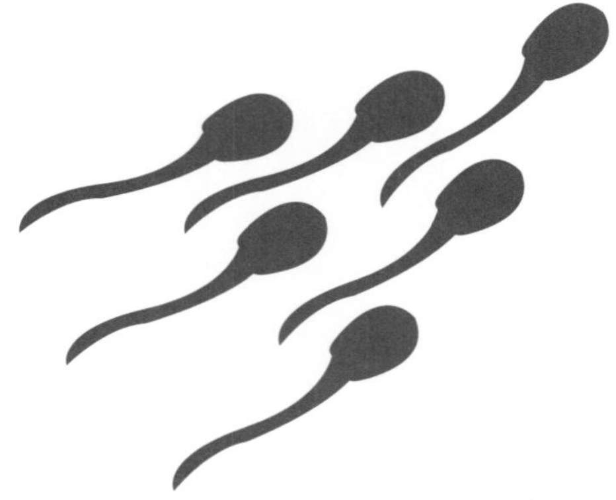

THE AVERAGE SPEED OF AN EJACULATION IS 28 MILES PER HOUR

THE VIBRATOR WAS ORIGINALLY INVENTED IN THE 19TH CENTURY TO TREAT 'FEMALE HYSTERIA'

SPOT THE DIFFERENCE – THERE'S ONLY ONE!

YOU'VE DROPPED YOUR DOUBLE-ENDED DILDO IN YOUR FRUIT AND VEG DRAWER! QUICK, FIND IT BEFORE GRAN COMES TO TEA!

YOU HAVE
15 SECONDS

FIND THIS PAIR ON THE OPPOSITE PAGE

... WHILE YOU SCREW

WOMEN NEED A REASON TO HAVE SEX, MEN JUST NEED A PLACE

BILLY CRYSTAL

WELCOME TO

WET BEAVER CREEK

A) AUSTRALIA

B) CANADA

C) USA

YOU HAVE 15 SECONDS

FIND LOVE

L E O V L E E V O E L O E V E
O L E L O E V V L E L E O O E
E O L E L O E L E O E V E L V
V L E O E V E L E V L L E O E
L E V E O L O E V L E V O E L
V L E O V E V E L O L E V L O
L E V E O L V O E L E V O V L
E L O V L E V O E O V E V L E
E L E O V L E E V O E L O E L
V O L E L O E V V L O V E O O
E E O L E L O E L E V E V E L
L V L E O E V E L O V O L E O
O L E V E O L O E V L E V O E
L V L E O V E V E L O L E V L
E L E V E O L V O E L E V O V

COLOUR THESE CUFFS

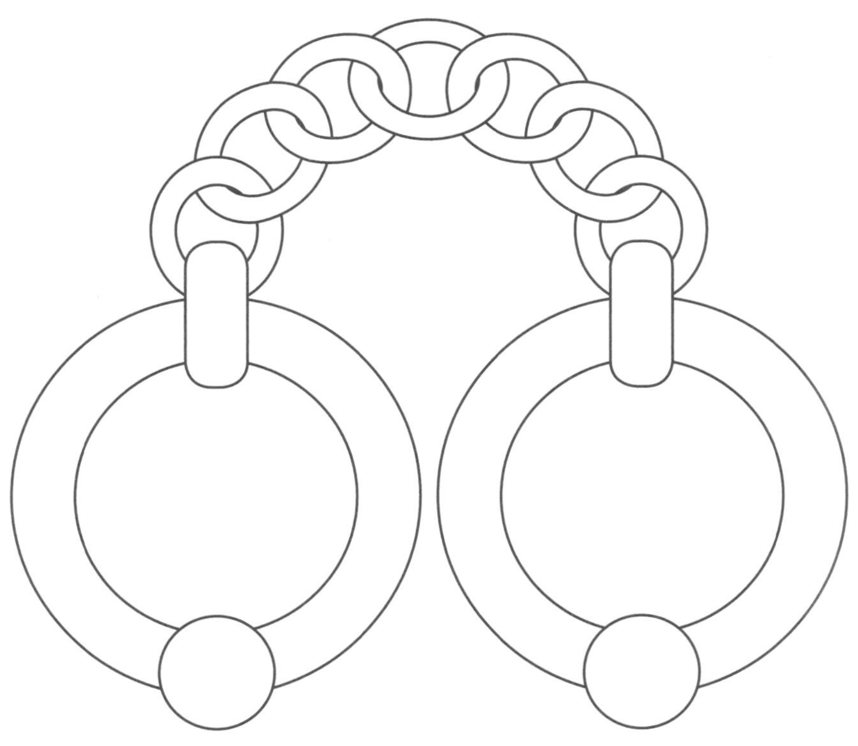

VAGINA
PUSSY
TWAT
BEAVER
MUFF
SNATCH
BOX
FANNY
MINGE
PUNANI
VADGE

V W E Y T R T A M N

Z V A G I N A X C B

A P S D F G W H J K

M U F F I O T E P L

Y S A X M I N G E P

T S N A T C H D B U

R Y N D S A E A O N

W X Y F G H J V X A

M B E A V E R K L N

N B V C Z A S D F I

YOU HAVE 15 SECONDS

FIND THIS PAIR ON THE OPPOSITE PAGE

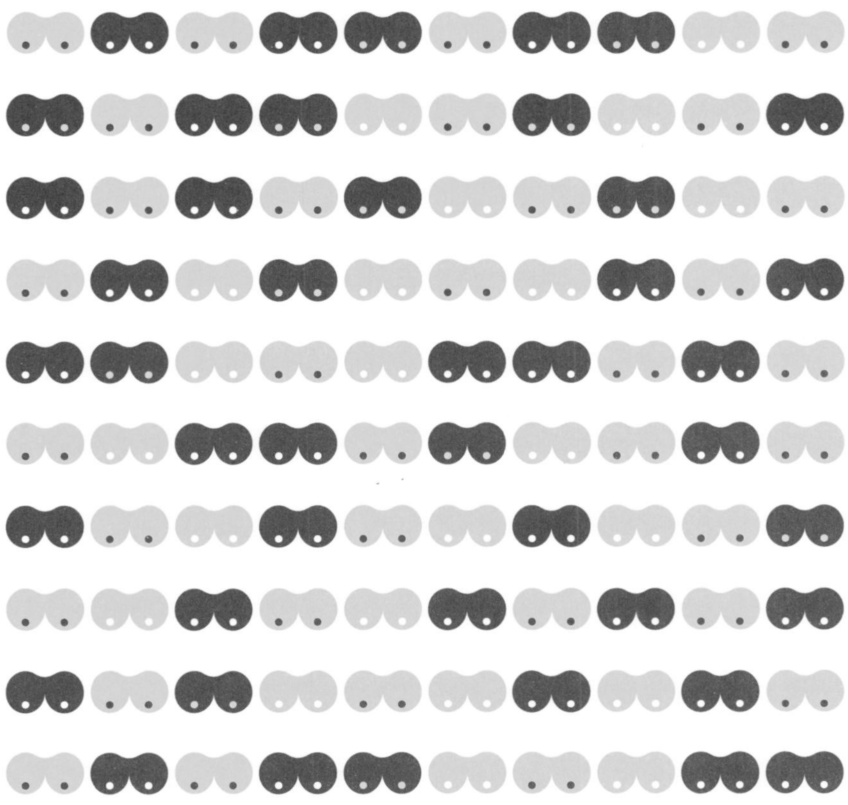

SCREW FACT

A MAN'S LEFT TESTICLE – WHICH IS ON THE RIGHT IF YOU'RE LOOKING STRAIGHT ON – TENDS TO HANG LOWER THAN HIS RIGHT ONE

SCREW FACT

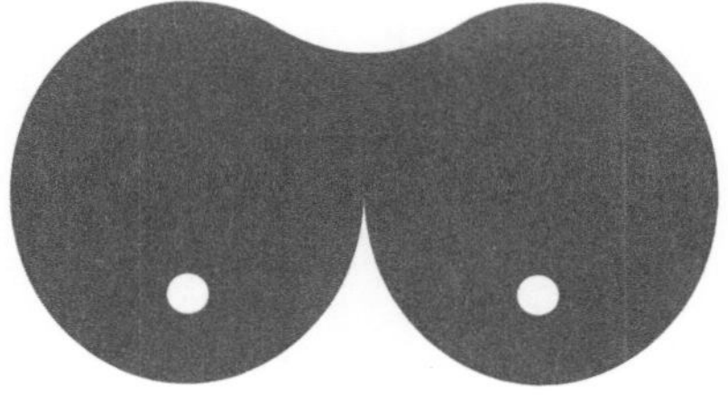

AROUND 1% OF WOMEN CAN REACH ORGASM SOLELY THROUGH STIMULATING THEIR BREASTS

FIND THE MIRROR IMAGE

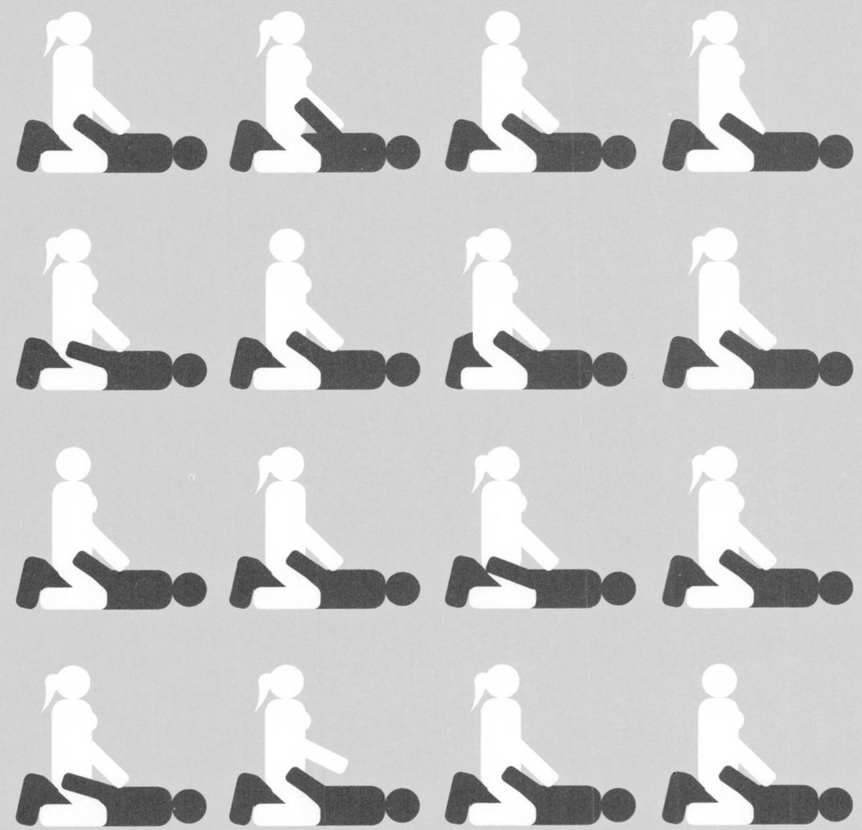

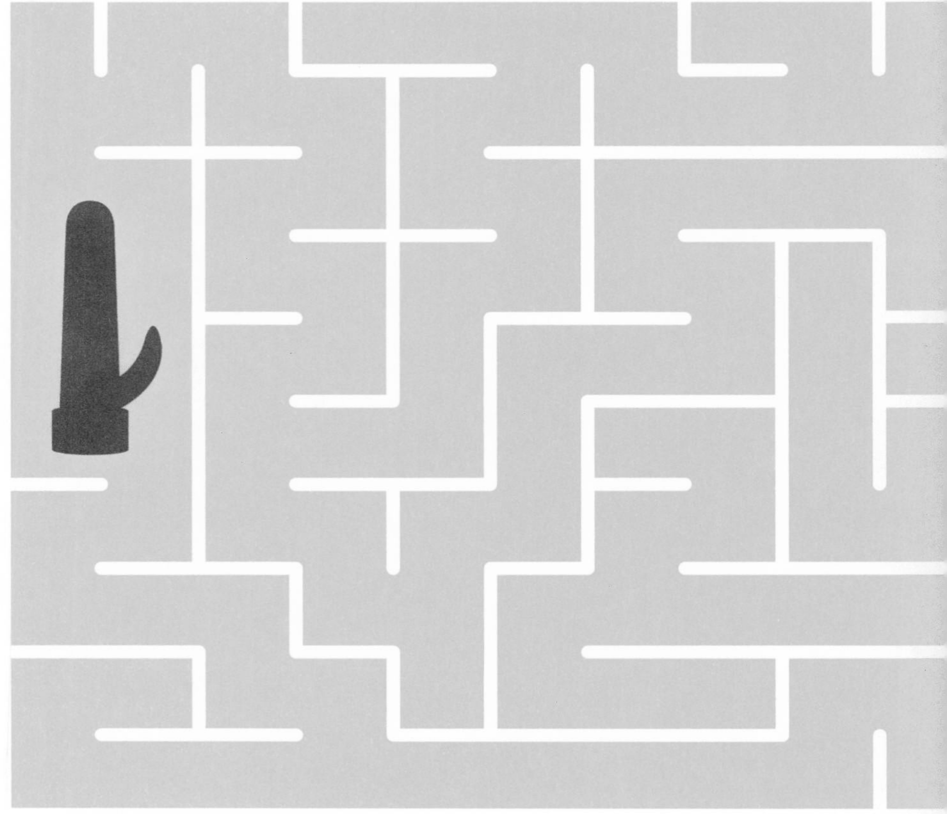

THE BEST TIME OF DAY FOR SEX IS ANYTIME BECAUSE IT'S SEX

CAMERON DIAZ

WELCOME TO

WANKUM

A) AUSTRIA

B) GERMANY

C) BELGIUM

YOU HAVE
15 SECONDS

FIND THIS PAIR ON THE OPPOSITE PAGE

69

FIND THE MAGIC NUMBER

96 99 66 96 99 66 66 99 99

66 99 96 66 99 96 99 66

96 66 66 96 66 99 99

66 99 99 66 96 96 96 66 96 96

96 99 66 96 99 66 66 99 99 96

66 99 96 66 99 96 99 66 99 66

96 66 66 66 96 66 96 99

99 66 66 96 96 66 96 66 96 96 96

96 99 66 96 99 66 66 99 99 96

66 99 96 66 99 96 99 66 66 99

96 66 96 66 66 99 66 69 99 99 66

SHOW YOUR CREATIVE FLAIR WITH PUBIC HAIR

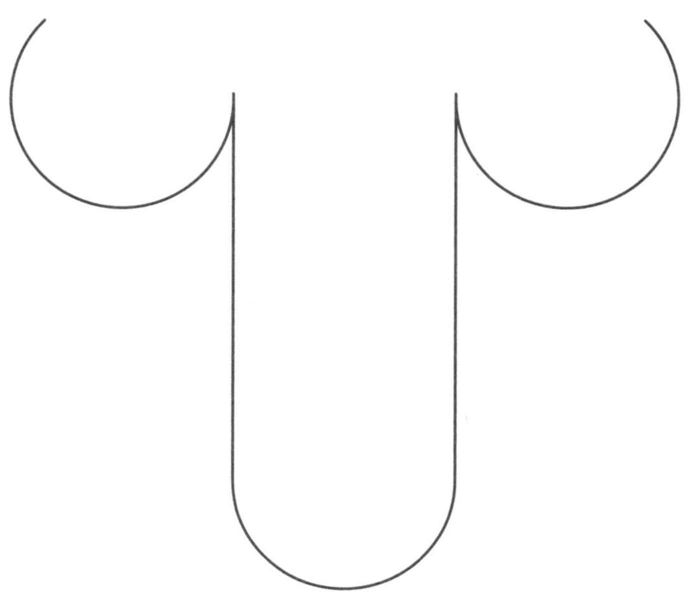

AMONG MEN, SEX SOMETIMES RESULTS IN INTIMACY; AMONG WOMEN, INTIMACY SOMETIMES RESULTS IN SEX

BARBARA CARTLAND

WELCOME TO

FANNY STREET

A) WALES

B) NEW ZEALAND

C) IRELAND

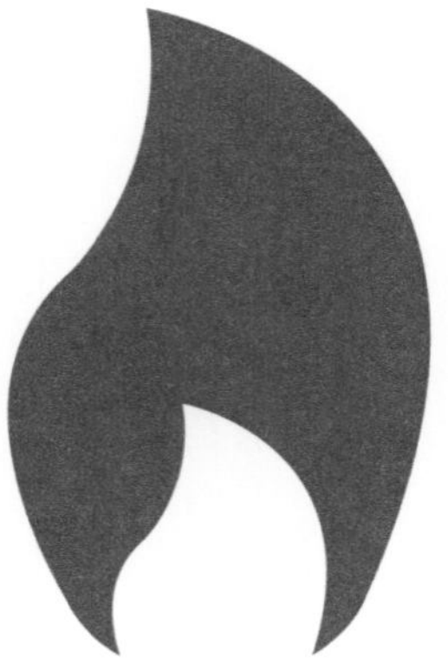

ON AVERAGE, MEN BURN AROUND 100 CALORIES DURING SEX, AND WOMEN BURN 69

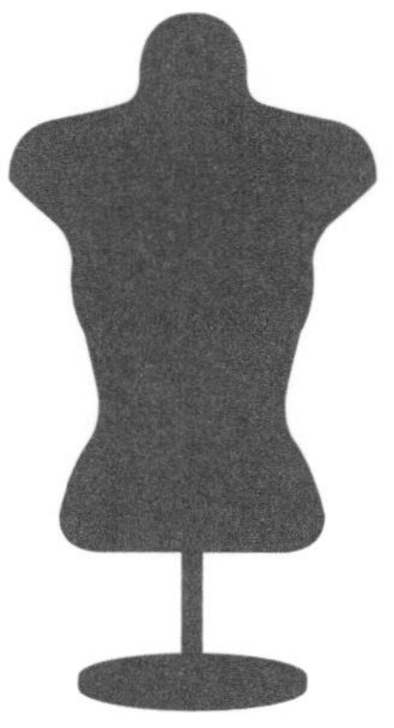

AGALMATOPHILIA IS THE SEXUAL ATTRACTION TO MANNEQUINS, DOLLS AND STATUES

MISSIONARY
DOGGIE
RIDE
COWGIRL
PLOUGH
SPOONS
LOTUS
SIDEWINDER
WATERFALL
SCISSORS

M	L	O	T	U	S	S	D	S	F
N	L	B	V	C	P	A	P	I	R
C	A	G	S	H	O	J	L	D	I
O	F	K	C	L	O	P	O	E	D
W	R	O	I	I	N	U	U	W	E
G	E	Y	S	T	S	R	G	I	E
I	T	C	S	V	B	N	H	N	W
R	A	D	O	G	G	I	E	D	M
L	W	A	R	S	D	F	G	E	H
M	I	S	S	I	O	N	A	R	Y

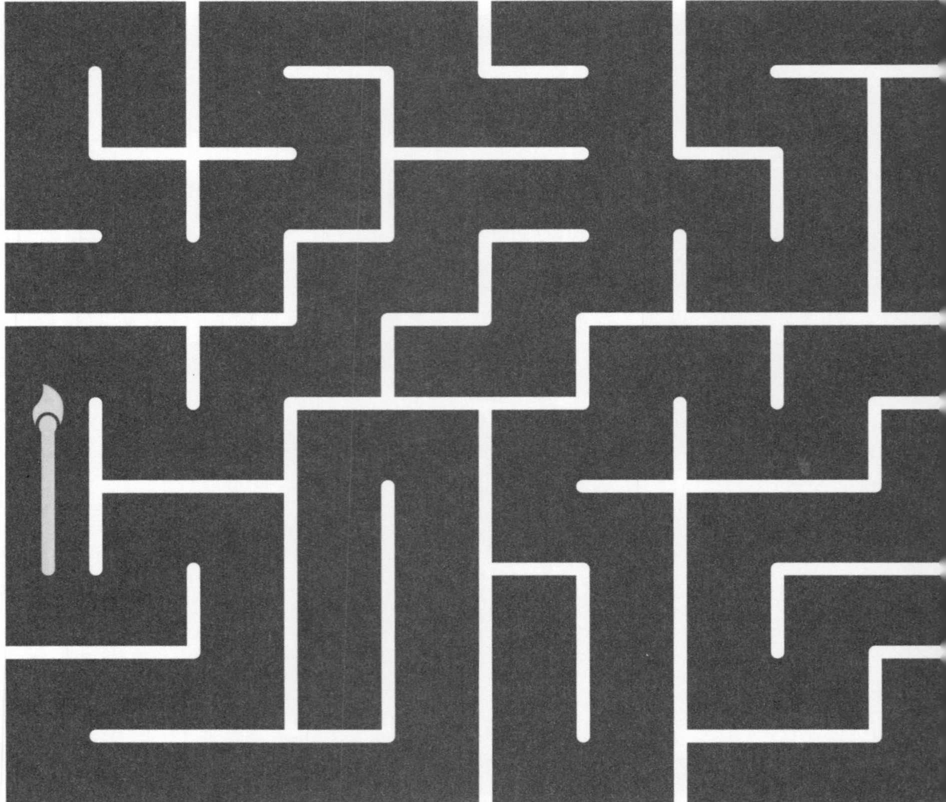

YOU HAVE
15 SECONDS

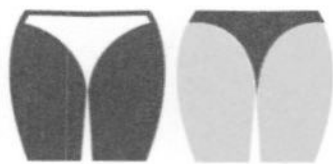

FIND THIS PAIR ON THE OPPOSITE PAGE

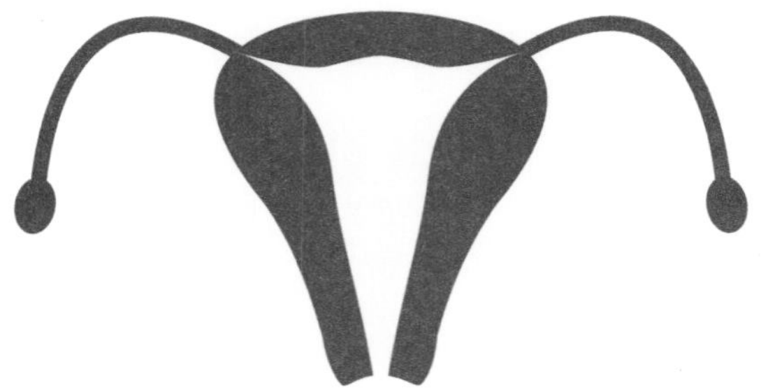

MEN ARE SUBCONSCIOUSLY MORE ATTRACTED TO A WOMAN DURING THE TIME SHE IS OVULATING

RESEARCH SUGGESTS THAT IT'S EASIER TO REACH ORGASM WHEN YOUR FEET ARE WARM

YOU'VE DROPPED THE KEY TO YOUR FLUFFY HANDCUFFS DOWN THE BACK OF THE SOFA. FIND IT TO RELEASE YOUR DATE!

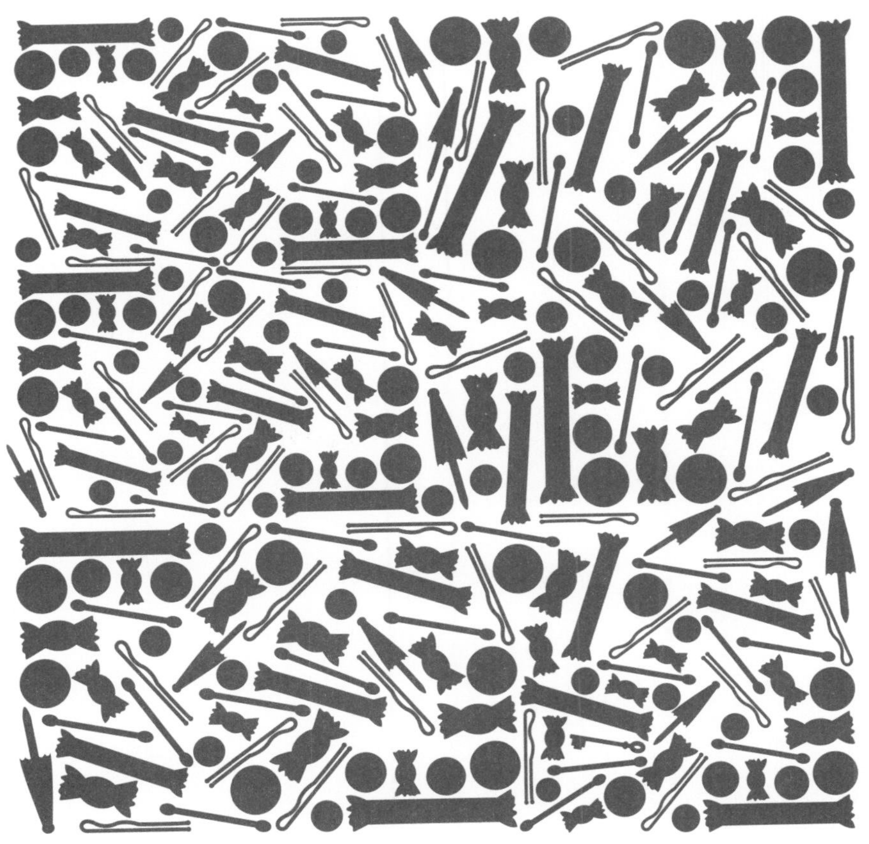

SEX: THE THING THAT TAKES UP THE LEAST AMOUNT OF TIME AND CAUSES THE MOST AMOUNT OF TROUBLE

JOHN BARRYMORE

WELCOME TO DILDO

A) CANADA

B) FRANCE

C) SCOTLAND

SPOT THE DIFFERENCE – THERE'S ONLY ONE!

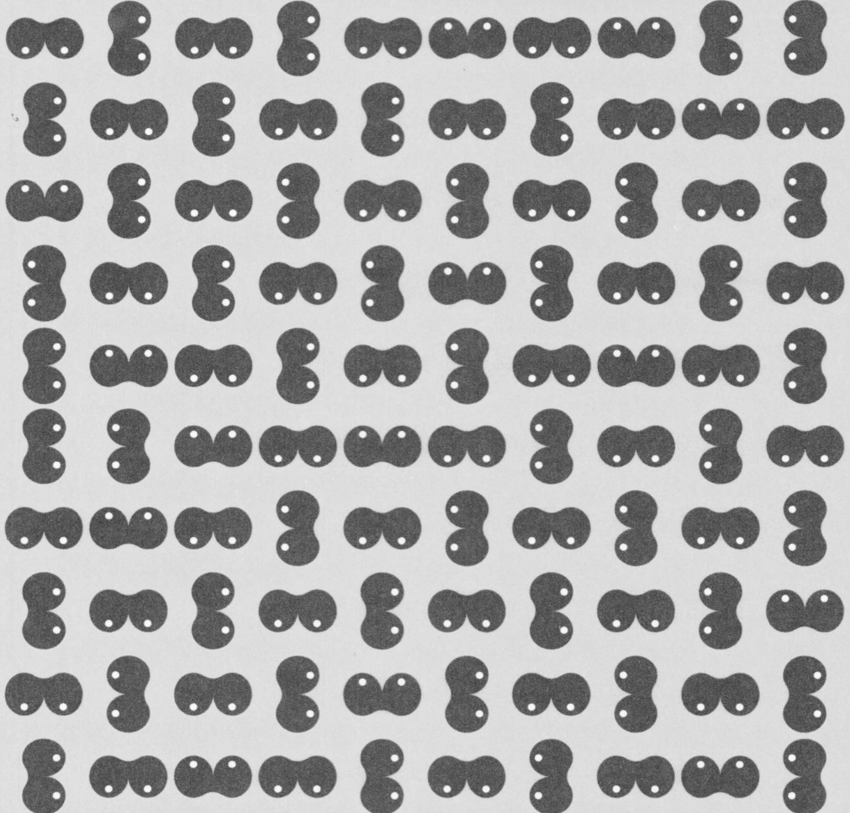

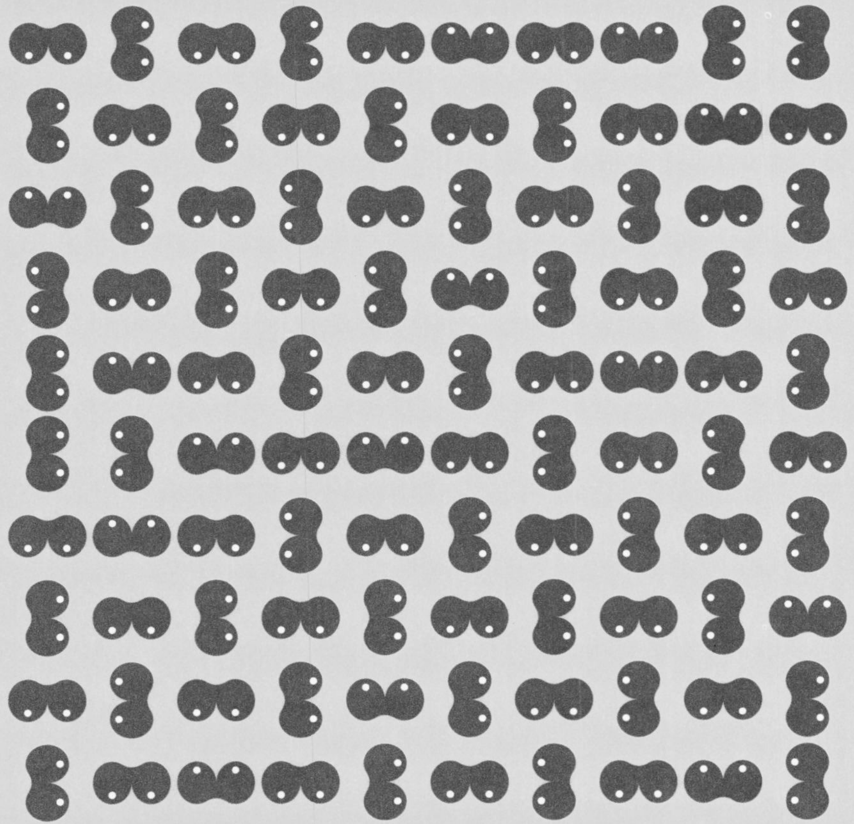

FIND THIS PAIR ON THE OPPOSITE PAGE

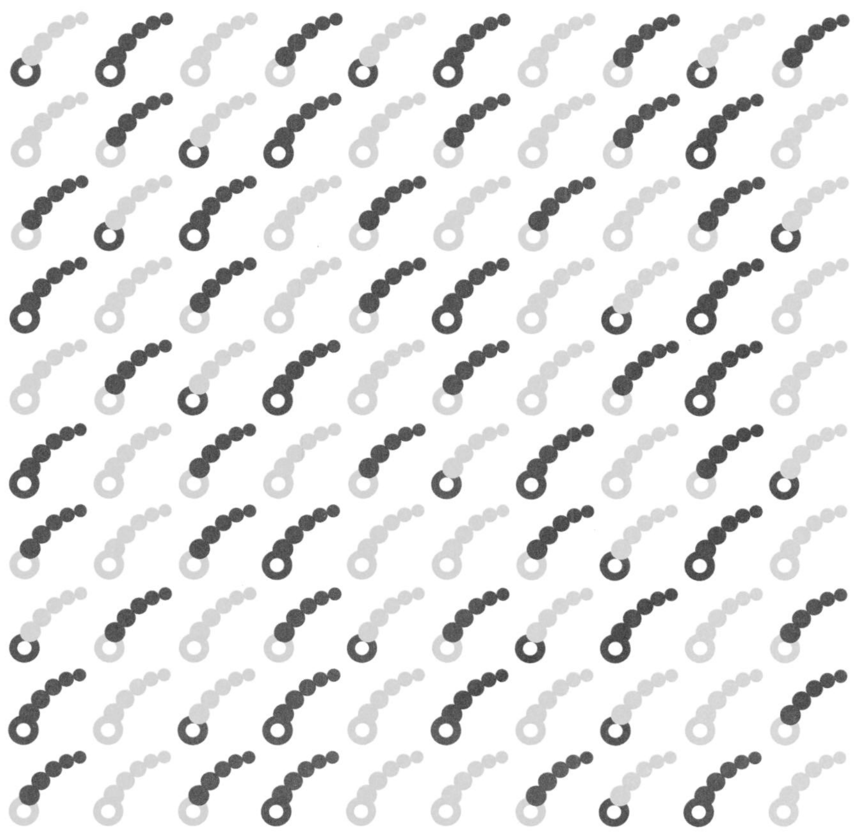

DECORATE THIS DILDO

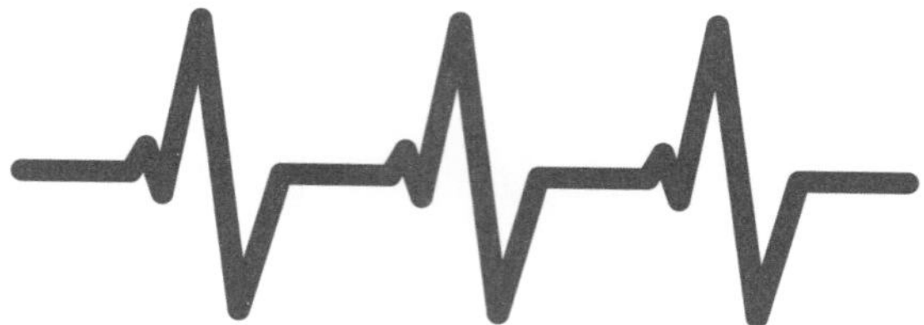

SEX REDUCES STRESS, LOWERS BLOOD PRESSURE AND BOOSTS YOUR IMMUNE SYSTEM

DURING SEX YOUR INNER NOSE SWELLS JUST LIKE YOUR BREAST TISSUE AND GENITALS DO

YOU CAN DO IT! FIND THE G-SPOT

G-STOP G-STOP G-SPTO G-STOP G-STOP G-SPTO G-STOP
G-SOPT G-STOP G-SOPT G-STOP G-STOP G-SPTO G-STOP
G-SPTO G-SPTO G-SPTO G-SPTO G-SPTO G-SPTO G-SPTO G-STOP
G-STOP G-STOP G-STOP G-SPTO G-STOP G-SPTO G-SPTO G-SPTO G-SPTO
G-SPTO G-STOP G-STOP G-STOP G-STOP G-SPTO G-SPTO G-STOP G-SPTO G-STOP
G-STOP G-STOP G-SPTO G-STOP G-STOP G-SPTO G-STOP
G-SOPT G-SPOT G-SOPT G-STOP G-STOP G-SPTO G-STOP
G-SPTO G-SPTO G-SPTO G-SPTO G-SPTO G-SPTO G-SPTO G-STOP
G-STOP G-STOP G-SPTO G-STOP G-SPTO G-SPTO G-SPTO G-SPTO
G-SPTO G-STOP
G-SPTO G-SPTO G-SPTO G-STOP G-STOP G-SPTO G-SPTO G-STOP G-SPTO
G-SOPT G-STOP G-SOPT G-STOP G-STOP G-SPTO G-STOP
G-SPTO G-SPTO G-SPTO G-SPTO G-SPTO G-SPTO G-SPTO G-STOP
G-STOP G-STOP G-SPTO G-STOP G-SPTO G-SPTO G-SPTO G-SPTO
G-SPTO G-SPTO G-STOP G-SPTO G-STOP G-STOP G-SPTO
G-STOP G-STOP G-SPTO G-STOP G-STOP G-SPTO G-STOP
G-SOPT G-STOP G-SOPT G-STOP G-STOP G-SPTO G-STOP
G-SPTO G-SPTO G-SPTO G-SPTO G-SPTO G-SPTO G-SPTO G-STOP
G-STOP G-STOP G-STOP G-SPTO G-STOP G-SPTO G-SPTO G-SPTO G-SPTO
G-SPTO G-STOP G-STOP G-STOP G-STOP G-SPTO G-SPTO G-STOP G-SPTO G-STOP
G-STOP G-STOP G-SPTO G-STOP G-STOP G-SPTO G-STOP
G-SOPT G-STOP G-SOPT G-STOP G-STOP G-SPTO G-STOP
G-SPTO G-SPTO G-SPTO G-SPTO G-SPTO G-SPTO G-SPTO G-STOP
G-STOP G-STOP G-SPTO G-STOP G-SPTO G-SPTO G-SPTO G-SPTO
G-SPTO G-STOP G-STOP G-STOP G-STOP G-STOP G-SPTO

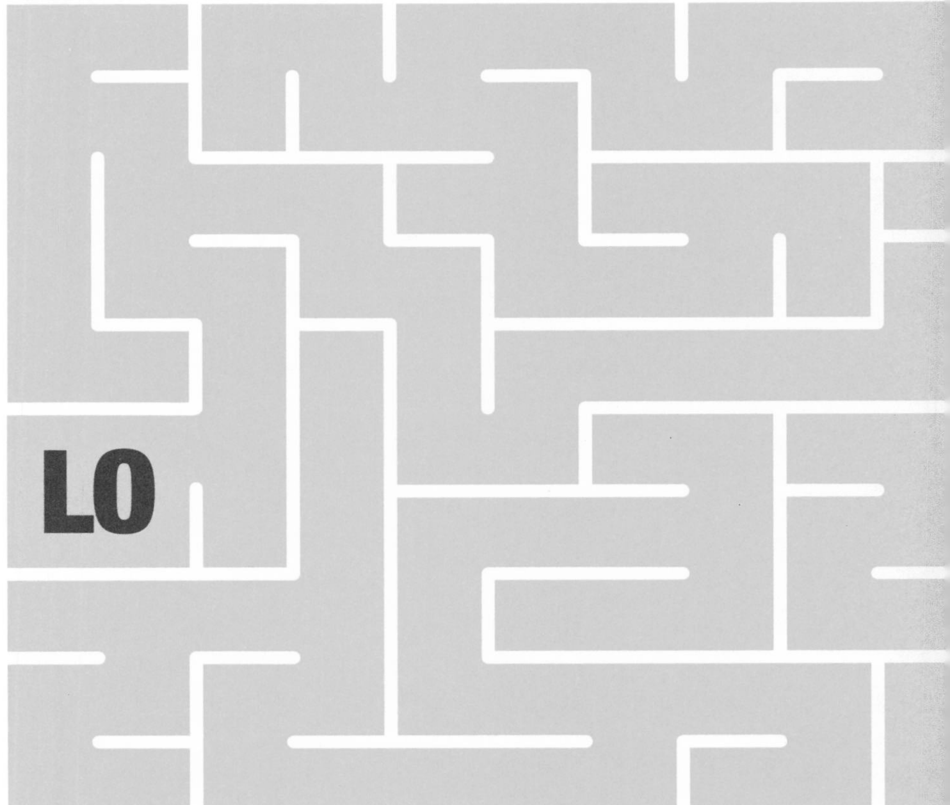
LO

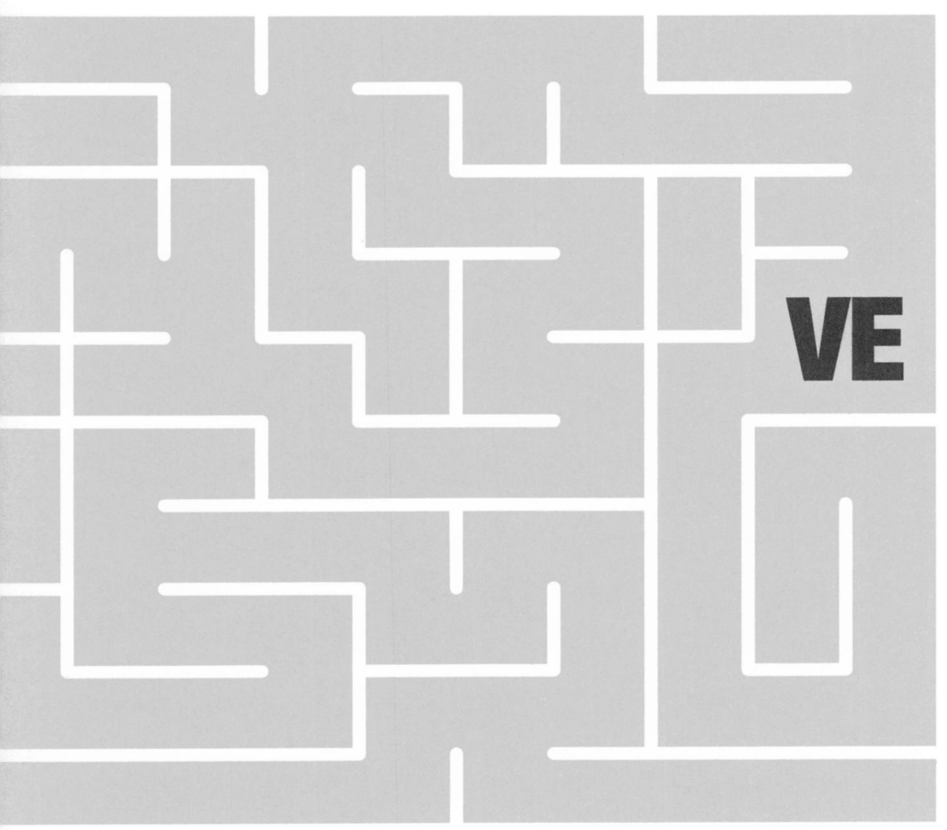
VE

SCREW

SHAG

BONK

BANG

POKE

COPULATE

GET LAID

HUMP

FORNICATE

MOUNT

BONE

W G E T L A I D C D
B S H A G N M K J H
C A B S D F G H C U
V B O N M P L P O M
B A N G O O I U P P
O W K E R K W T U Y
N A S D F E E G L H
E U I O P L R K A J
Y F O R N I C A T E
T M O U N T S R E E

... WHILE YOU SCREW

**SEX IS PART OF NATURE.
I GO ALONG WITH NATURE.**

MARILYN MONROE

WELCOME TO

COCKBUSH AVENUE

A) SINGAPORE

B) SOUTH AFRICA

C) ENGLAND

LET'S GET 'KINKY'

KIKNY KNYKI KYNKI KIKNY KNYKI KYNKI KYNKI KIKNY
KYNKI KIKNY KYNKI KIKNY KYNKI KIKNY KYNKI
KIKNY KNYKI KYNKI KYNKI KIKNY KYNKI KIKNY
KYNKI KIKNY KYNKI KIKNY
KYNKI KIKNY KIKNY KYNKI KYNKI KNYKI KIKNY KYNKI
KIKNY KNYKI KYNKI KIKNY KNYKI KYNKI KYNKI KIKNY
KYNKI KIKNY KYNKI KIKNY KYNKI KIKNY KYNKI
KIKNY KNYKI KYNKI KYNKI KIKNY KYNKI KIKNY
KYNKI KIKNY KYNKI KYNKI KNYKI KIKNY KYNKI
KYNKI KIKNY KYNKI KYNKI KIKNY KYNKI KIKNY
KYNKI KIKNY KYNKI KIKNY KYNKI KYNKI KNYKI KIKNY KYNKI
KYNKI KIKNY KIKNY
KIKNY KNYKI KYNKI KIKNY KNYKI KYNKI KYNKI KIKNY
KYNKI KIKNY KYNKI KIKNY KYNKI KIKNY KYNKI
KIKNY KNYKI KYNKI KYNKI KIKNY KYNKI KIKNY
KYNKI KIKNY KYNKI KIKNY
KYNKI KIKNY KIKNY KYNKI KYNKI KNYKI KIKNY KYNKI
KIKNY KNYKI KYNKI KIKNY KNYKI KYNKI KYNKI KIKNY
KYNKI KIKNY KYNKI KIKNY KYNKI KIKNY KYNKI
KINKY KNYKI KYNKI KIKNY KYNKI KIKNY
KYNKI KYNKI
KYNKI KYNKI KIKNY KYNKI KNYKI KYNKI KYNKI

SCREW FACT

PEOPLE WHO SLEEP FACE DOWN WITH THEIR ARMS STRETCHED ABOVE THEIR HEAD HAVE MORE SEXUAL DREAMS

SCREW FACT

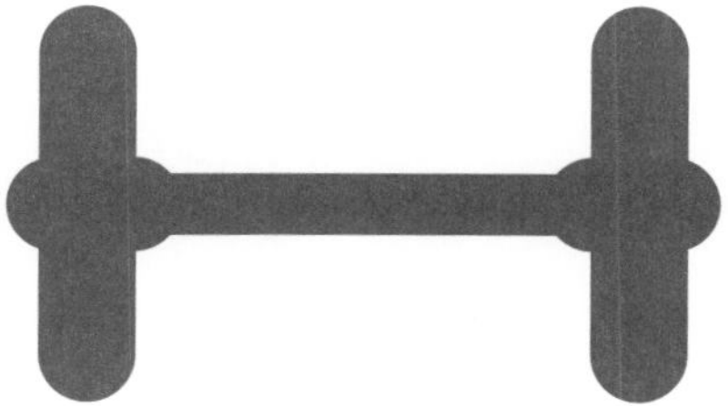

MORE BLOOD FLOWS TO YOUR GENITALS AFTER A GYM SESSION, AND TESTOSTERONE LEVELS INCREASE, SO IT'S A GOOD TIME FOR SEX

YOU HAVE 15 SECONDS

FIND THIS PAIR ON THE OPPOSITE PAGE

MIRROR POSITION

FIND THE MIRROR IMAGE

I NEED MORE SEX, OK? BEFORE I DIE I WANNA TASTE EVERYONE IN THE WORLD

ANGELINA JOLIE

WELCOME TO

LE TAMPON

A) FRANCE

B) QUEBEC

C) ALGERIA

SPOT THE DIFFERENCE – THERE'S ONLY ONE!

VIBRATOR
STRAP ON
BUTT PLUG
COCK RING
WHIP
HANDCUFFS
BLINDFOLD
BEADS
LOVE EGGS
DILDO

M	N	V	T	T	B	N	V	G	G
B	L	I	N	D	F	O	L	D	H
E	C	B	A	I	S	P	C	B	A
A	D	R	F	L	H	A	O	U	N
D	K	A	J	D	G	R	C	T	D
S	L	T	P	O	O	T	K	T	C
T	Y	O	T	U	I	S	R	P	U
R	E	R	W	A	S	D	I	L	F
J	G	G	W	H	I	P	N	U	F
E	F	L	O	V	E	E	G	G	S

SCREW FACT

25% OF PENISES ARE SLIGHTLY BENT WHEN ERECT

SCREW FACT

EVERY DAY ACROSS THE WORLD ROUGHLY 100 MILLION ACTS OF SEXUAL INTERCOURSE OCCUR

FIND THE CROTCH-LESS PANTIES

SHOW YOUR CREATIVE FLAIR WITH PUBIC HAIR

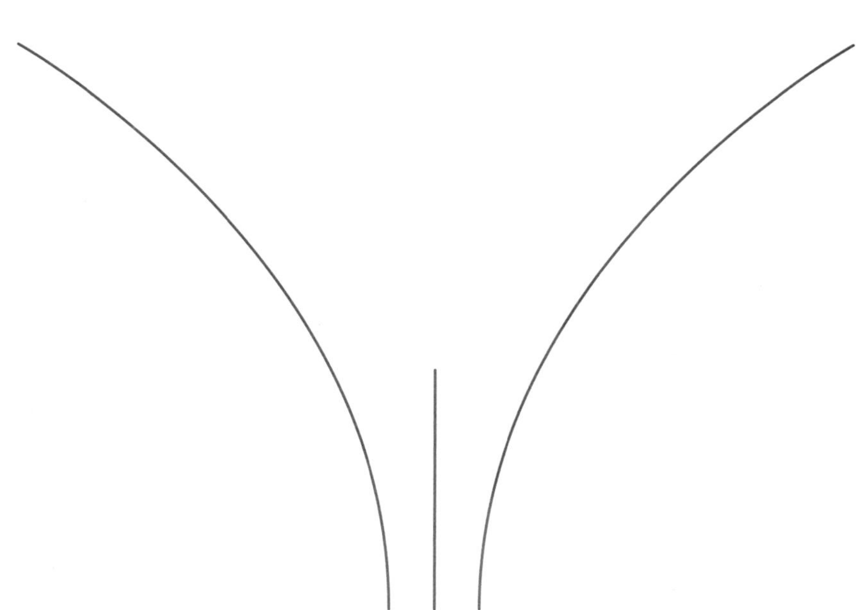

GOOD SEX IS LIKE GOOD BRIDGE – IF YOU DON'T HAVE A GOOD PARTNER, YOU'D BETTER HAVE A GOOD HAND

MAE WEST

ANSWERS

P6–7

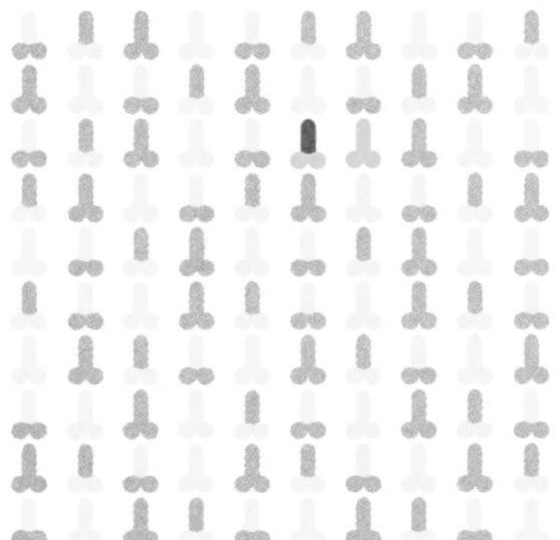

P12–13

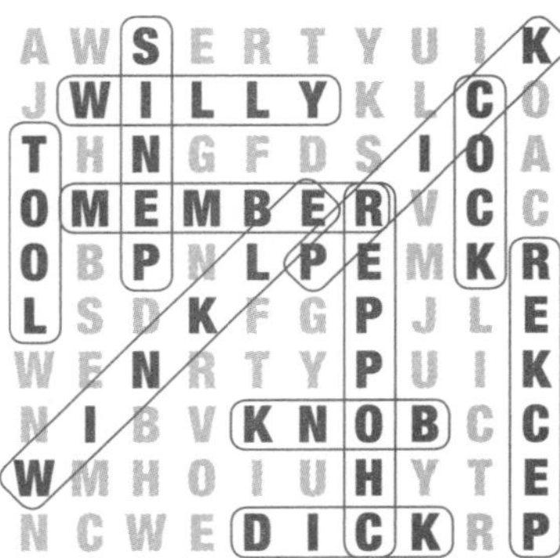

P8–9

P15 **A) CZECH REPUBLIC**

P16–17

P22–23

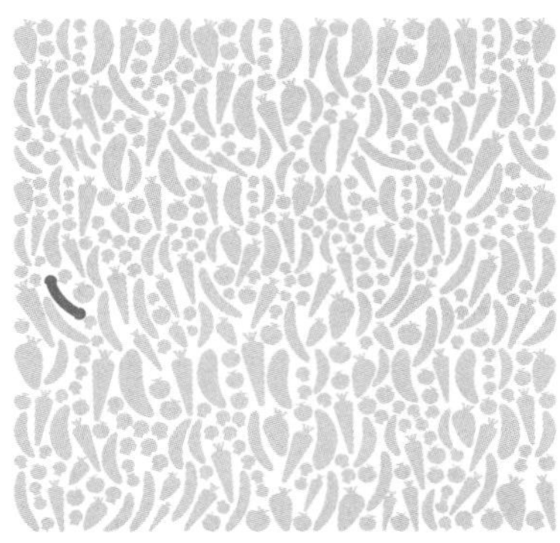

P20–21

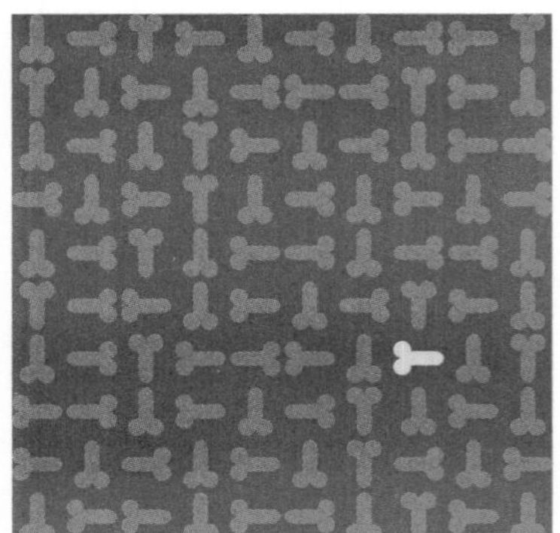

P24–25

P27 **C) USA**

P28–29

L E O V L E E V O E L O E V E
O L E L O E V V L E L E O O E
E O L E L O E L E O E V E L V
V L E O E V E L E V L L E O E
L E V E O L O E V L E V O E L
V L E O V E V E L O L E V L O
L E V E O L V O E L E V O V L
E L O V L E V O E O V E V L E
E L E O V L E E V O E L O E L
V O L E L O E V V **L O V E** O O
E E O L E E O E L E V E V E L
L V L E O E V E L O V O L E O
O L E V E O L O E V L E V O E
L V L E O V E V E L O L E V L
E L E V E O L V O E L E V O V

P32–33

P34–35

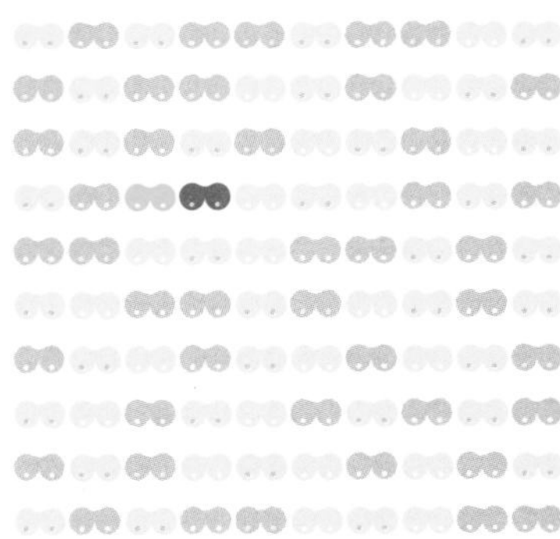

P38–39

P40–41

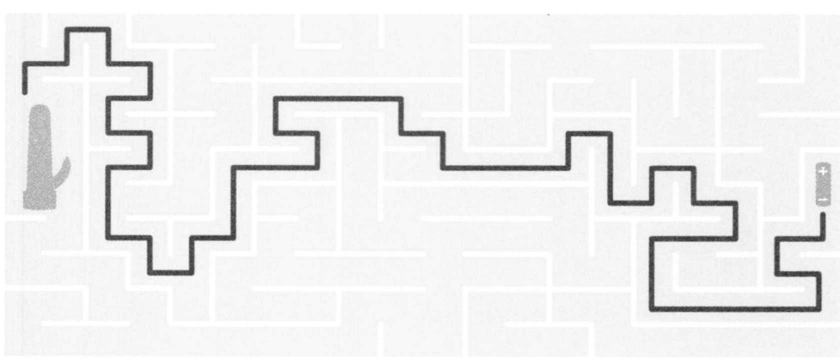

P43 **B) GERMANY**

P44–45

P46–47

P51 **A) WALES**

P54–55

P58–59

P56–57

P62–63

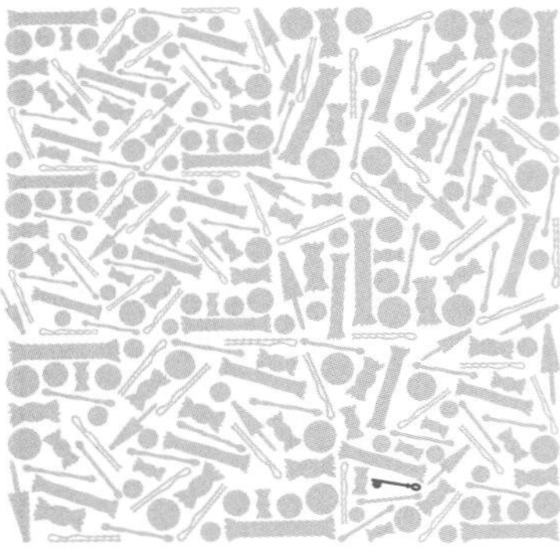

P68–69

P65 **A) CANADA**

P66–67

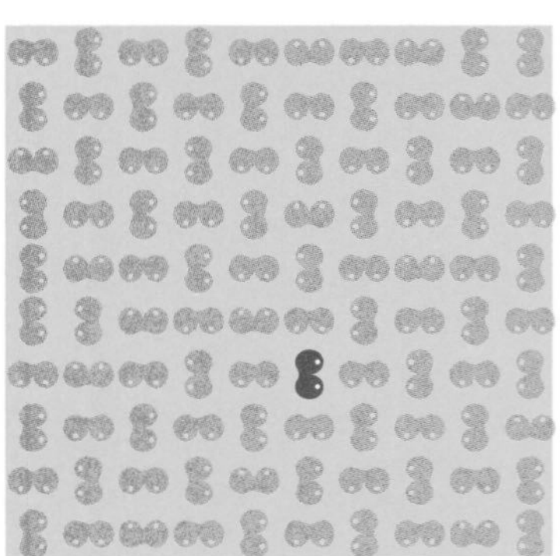

P74–75

G-STOP G-STOP G-SPTO G-STOP G-STOP G-SPTO G-STOP
G-SOPT G-STOP G-SOPT G-STOP G-STOP G-SPTO G-STOP
G-SPTO G-SPTO G-SPTO G-SPTO G-STOP G-SPTO G-SPTO G-STOP
G-STOP G-STOP G-STOP G-SPTO G-STOP G-SPTO G-SPTO G-SPTO G-SPTO
G-SPTO G-STOP G-STOP G-STOP G-STOP G-SPTO G-SPTO G-STOP G-SPTO G-STOP
G-STOP G-STOP G-SPTO G-STOP G-STOP G-SPTO G-STOP
G-SOPT **G-SPOT** G-SOPT G-STOP G-STOP G-SPTO G-STOP
G-SPTO G-SPTO G-SPTO G-SPTO G-STOP G-SPTO G-SPTO G-STOP
G-STOP G-STOP G-SPTO G-STOP G-SPTO G-SPTO G-SPTO G-SPTO
G-SPTO G-SPTO G-SPTO G-SPTO G-STOP G-STOP G-SPTO G-STOP G-SPTO G-STOP G-SPTO
G-SOPT G-STOP G-SOPT G-STOP G-STOP G-SPTO G-STOP
G-SPTO G-SPTO G-SPTO G-SPTO G-STOP G-SPTO G-SPTO G-STOP
G-STOP G-STOP G-SPTO G-STOP G-SPTO G-SPTO G-SPTO G-SPTO
G-SPTO G-SPTO G-STOP G-SPTO G-STOP G-STOP G-SPTO
G-STOP G-STOP G-SPTO G-STOP G-STOP G-SPTO G-STOP
G-SOPT G-STOP G-SOPT G-STOP G-STOP G-SPTO G-STOP
G-SPTO G-SPTO G-SPTO G-SPTO G-STOP G-SPTO G-SPTO G-STOP
G-STOP G-STOP G-STOP G-SPTO G-STOP G-SPTO G-SPTO G-SPTO G-SPTO
G-SPTO G-STOP G-STOP G-STOP G-STOP G-SPTO G-SPTO G-STOP G-SPTO G-STOP
G-STOP G-STOP G-SPTO G-STOP G-STOP G-SPTO G-STOP
G-SOPT G-STOP G-SOPT G-STOP G-STOP G-SPTO G-STOP
G-SPTO G-SPTO G-SPTO G-SPTO G-STOP G-SPTO G-SPTO G-STOP
G-STOP G-STOP G-SPTO G-STOP G-SPTO G-SPTO G-SPTO G-SPTO
G-SPTO G-STOP G-STOP G-STOP G-STOP G-STOP G-SPTO

P76–77

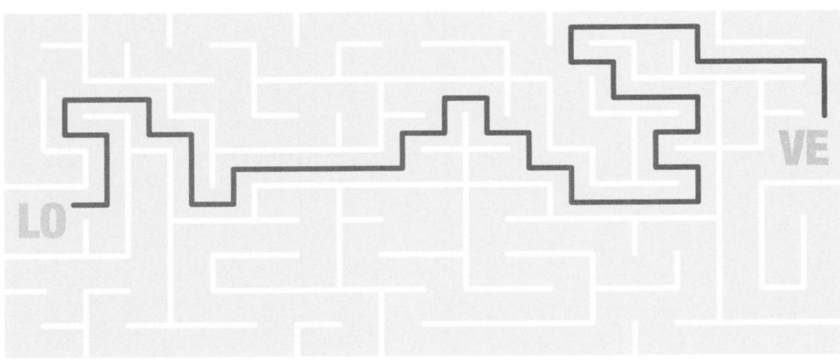

P78–79

P81 **C) ENGLAND**

P82–83

KINKY

P86–87

P88–89

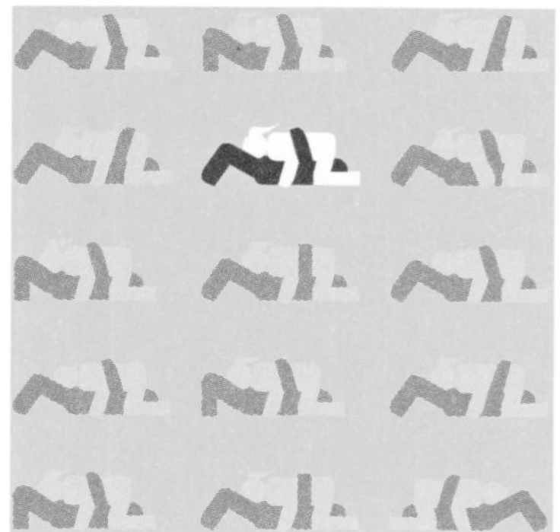

P91 **A) FRANCE**

P92–93

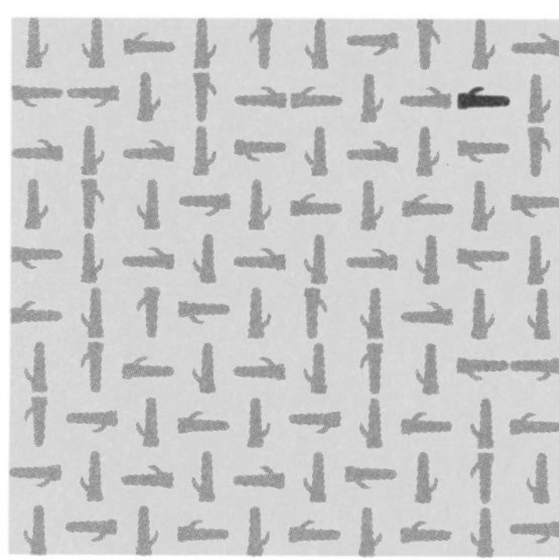

P94–95

M	N	V	T	T	B	N	V	G	G
B	L	I	N	D	F	O	L	D	H
E	C	B	A	I	S	P	C	B	A
A	D	R	F	L	H	A	O	U	N
D	K	A	J	D	G	R	C	T	D
S	L	T	P	O	O	T	K	T	C
T	Y	O	T	U	I	S	R	P	U
R	E	R	W	A	S	D	I	L	F
J	G	G	W	H	I	P	N	U	F
E	F	L	O	V	E	E	G	G	S

P98–99

IF YOU'RE INTERESTED IN FINDING OUT MORE ABOUT OUR BOOKS, FIND US ON FACEBOOK AT SUMMERSDALE PUBLISHERS AND FOLLOW US ON TWITTER AT @SUMMERSDALE.

WWW.SUMMERSDALE.COM